Frances Lincoln Limited, an imprint of The Quarto Group
The Old Brewery, 6 Blundell Street,
London N7 9BH

www.QuartoKnows.com

The Royal Horticultural Society A Gardener's Five Year Record Book
Copyright © Frances Lincoln Limited 2017

An interest in gardening is all you need to enjoy being a member
of the RHS. rhs.org.uk

First Frances Lincoln edition

A catalogue record for this book is available from the British Library

978-0-7112-3869-5

Printed in China

9 8 7 6 5

Quarto is the authority on a wide range of topics.

Quarto educates, entertains and enriches the lives of
our readers – enthusiasts and lovers of hands-on living.

www.QuartoKnows.com

RHS Flower Show information can be found by visiting rhs.org.uk

INTRODUCTION

The decorations in this book are all taken from illustrations housed in the RHS Lindley Library, and give a good indication of the range of images the Library holds.

First of all, there are printed illustrations, whether from books or nursery catalogues, made using a variety of techniques. There are hand-coloured engravings from the eighteenth and nineteenth centuries, the earliest used date from the 1770s: engraved copies of Chinese drawings of plants, compiled by Pierre-Joseph Buc'hoz in his *Collection précieuse et enluminée des fleurs* (1775). The following decade gives us Johann Simon Kerner's work on trees and shrubs, and James Bolton's treatise on British ferns, the *Filices Britannicae*. The most famous are Pierre-Joseph Redouté's great work on roses, published between 1817 and 1825. Also, too little known today, are some images published by Buc'hoz in the 1780s, based on Chinese paintings of plants. There are coloured lithographs from the nineteenth century, especially from Valentine Bartholomew's 1821 *Selection of Flowers*, printed by the pioneering English lithographer Charles Hullmandel; Bartholomew drew directly onto the lithographic stone, and so did not have to let his drawing be interpreted by an engraver. There are also some splendid images from the catalogues of the Yokohama Nursery Company, showing the best in Japanese lithography at the turn of the twentieth century.

You will also notice that a couple of insects have crept into the foliage and flowers: a bumblebee from John Curtis's *British Entomology* (1823-40), and a beetle by E. W. Robinson.

There are also many details taken from original drawings in the Society's collection, including the earliest volume of drawings the RHS possesses: a florilegium, probably dating from the 1630s, by Pieter van Kouwenhoorn, who was obviously preparing his volume of plant portraits for publication. There is an adonis by an artist of the next generation, Pieter van Holsteyn; herbs and vegetables from a remarkable pair of Belgian volumes from the end of the eighteenth century; and flowers from an anonymous French two-volume work of the early 1800s entitled *Flore du desert*. There are fruit portraits by William Hooker, who was hired by the Horticultural Society as its first artist. Female flower painters of the nineteenth century include Caroline Maria Applebee and Lydia Penrose, succeeded by Lilian Snelling, who in the twentieth century became the principal illustrator for *Curtis's Botanical Magazine*. Illustrations by Cynthia Newsome-Taylor and Graham Stuart Thomas bring us to the present day. But there are also drawings by Chinese and Japanese artists, for the most part anonymous.

Brent Elliott
Historian, RHS Lindley Library

YEAR		
WEATHER		
PLANTS IN BLOOM		
TASKS		
NOTES		

JANUARY

YEAR

WEATHER

PLANTS IN BLOOM

TASKS

NOTES

JANUARY

YEAR

WEATHER

PLANTS IN BLOOM

TASKS

NOTES

JANUARY

YEAR

WEATHER

PLANTS IN BLOOM

TASKS

NOTES

JANUARY

YEAR		
WEATHER		
PLANTS IN BLOOM		
TASKS		
NOTES		

JANUARY

YEAR		
WEATHER		
PLANTS IN BLOOM		
TASKS		
NOTES		

FEBRUARY

YEAR

WEATHER

PLANTS IN BLOOM

TASKS

NOTES

FEBRUARY

YEAR		
WEATHER		
PLANTS IN BLOOM		
TASKS		
NOTES		

FEBRUARY

YEAR

WEATHER

PLANTS IN BLOOM

TASKS

NOTES

FEBRUARY

YEAR		
WEATHER		
PLANTS IN BLOOM		
TASKS		
NOTES		

FEBRUARY

YEAR		
WEATHER		
PLANTS IN BLOOM		
TASKS		
NOTES		

MARCH

YEAR		
WEATHER		
PLANTS IN BLOOM		
TASKS		
NOTES		

MARCH

YEAR

WEATHER

PLANTS IN BLOOM

TASKS

NOTES

MARCH

YEAR		
WEATHER		
PLANTS IN BLOOM		
TASKS		
NOTES		

MARCH

YEAR		
WEATHER		
PLANTS IN BLOOM		
TASKS		
NOTES		

MARCH

YEAR

WEATHER

PLANTS IN BLOOM

TASKS

NOTES

APRIL

YEAR

WEATHER

PLANTS IN BLOOM

TASKS

NOTES

APRIL

YEAR

WEATHER

PLANTS IN BLOOM

TASKS

NOTES

APRIL

YEAR		
WEATHER		
PLANTS IN BLOOM		
TASKS		
NOTES		

APRIL

YEAR

WEATHER

PLANTS IN BLOOM

TASKS

NOTES

APRIL

YEAR

WEATHER

PLANTS IN BLOOM

TASKS

NOTES

MAY

YEAR

WEATHER

PLANTS IN BLOOM

TASKS

NOTES

MAY

YEAR		
WEATHER		
PLANTS IN BLOOM		
TASKS		
NOTES		

MAY

YEAR

WEATHER

PLANTS IN BLOOM

TASKS

NOTES

MAY

YEAR

WEATHER

PLANTS IN BLOOM

TASKS

NOTES

MAY

YEAR		
WEATHER		
PLANTS IN BLOOM		
TASKS		
NOTES		

JUNE

YEAR		
WEATHER		
PLANTS IN BLOOM		
TASKS		
NOTES		

JUNE

YEAR		
WEATHER		
PLANTS IN BLOOM		
TASKS		
NOTES		

JUNE

YEAR		
WEATHER		
PLANTS IN BLOOM		
TASKS		
NOTES		

JUNE

YEAR

WEATHER

PLANTS IN BLOOM

TASKS

NOTES

JUNE

YEAR		
WEATHER		
PLANTS IN BLOOM		
TASKS		
NOTES		

JULY

YEAR

WEATHER

PLANTS IN BLOOM

TASKS

NOTES

JULY

YEAR

WEATHER

PLANTS IN BLOOM

TASKS

NOTES

JULY

YEAR

WEATHER

PLANTS IN BLOOM

TASKS

NOTES

JULY

YEAR

WEATHER

PLANTS IN BLOOM

TASKS

NOTES

JULY

YEAR

WEATHER

PLANTS IN BLOOM

TASKS

NOTES

AUGUST

YEAR

WEATHER

PLANTS IN BLOOM

TASKS

NOTES

AUGUST

YEAR

WEATHER

PLANTS IN BLOOM

TASKS

NOTES

AUGUST

YEAR

WEATHER

PLANTS IN BLOOM

TASKS

NOTES

AUGUST

YEAR

WEATHER

PLANTS IN BLOOM

TASKS

NOTES

AUGUST

YEAR		
WEATHER		
PLANTS IN BLOOM		
TASKS		
NOTES		

SEPTEMBER

YEAR		
WEATHER		
PLANTS IN BLOOM		
TASKS		
NOTES		

SEPTEMBER

YEAR		
WEATHER		
PLANTS IN BLOOM		
TASKS		
NOTES		

SEPTEMBER

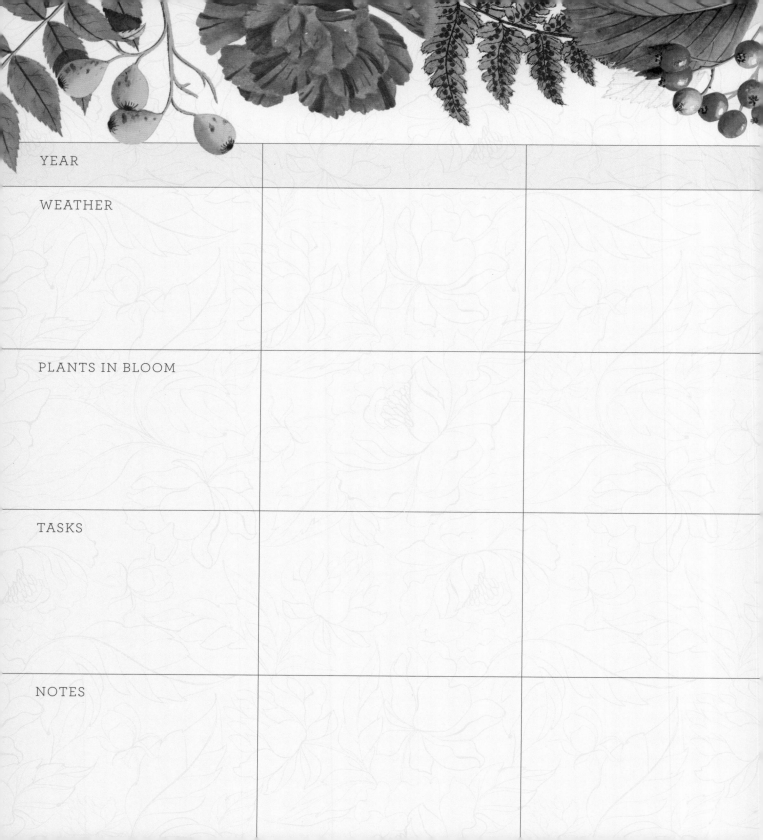

YEAR		
WEATHER		
PLANTS IN BLOOM		
TASKS		
NOTES		

SEPTEMBER

YEAR

WEATHER

PLANTS IN BLOOM

TASKS

NOTES

SEPTEMBER

YEAR		
WEATHER		
PLANTS IN BLOOM		
TASKS		
NOTES		

OCTOBER

YEAR

WEATHER

PLANTS IN BLOOM

TASKS

NOTES

OCTOBER

YEAR

WEATHER

PLANTS IN BLOOM

TASKS

NOTES

OCTOBER

YEAR		
WEATHER		
PLANTS IN BLOOM		
TASKS		
NOTES		

OCTOBER

YEAR		
WEATHER		
PLANTS IN BLOOM		
TASKS		
NOTES		

OCTOBER

YEAR		
WEATHER		
PLANTS IN BLOOM		
TASKS		
NOTES		

NOVEMBER

YEAR		
WEATHER		
PLANTS IN BLOOM		
TASKS		
NOTES		

NOVEMBER

YEAR		
WEATHER		
PLANTS IN BLOOM		
TASKS		
NOTES		

NOVEMBER

YEAR		
WEATHER		
PLANTS IN BLOOM		
TASKS		
NOTES		

NOVEMBER

YEAR		
WEATHER		
PLANTS IN BLOOM		
TASKS		
NOTES		

NOVEMBER

YEAR

WEATHER

PLANTS IN BLOOM

TASKS

NOTES

DECEMBER

YEAR		
WEATHER		
PLANTS IN BLOOM		
TASKS		
NOTES		

DECEMBER

YEAR

WEATHER

PLANTS IN BLOOM

TASKS

NOTES

DECEMBER

YEAR		
WEATHER		
PLANTS IN BLOOM		
TASKS		
NOTES		

DECEMBER

YEAR		
WEATHER		
PLANTS IN BLOOM		
TASKS		
NOTES		

DECEMBER

PLANT NAME	WHERE SEEN	SUPPLIER	PLANTING POSITION

PLANTS TO BUY

PLANT NAME	WHERE SEEN	SUPPLIER	PLANTING POSITION

PLANT NAME	WHERE SEEN	SUPPLIER	PLANTING POSITION

PLANTS TO BUY

PLANT NAME	WHERE SEEN	SUPPLIER	PLANTING POSITION

NAME	USEFUL ADDRESSES	TEL/EMAIL

PLANT SUPPLIERS

NAME	USEFUL ADDRESSES	TEL/EMAIL

NAME	USEFUL ADDRESSES	TEL/EMAIL

PLANT SUPPLIERS

NAME	USEFUL ADDRESSES	TEL/EMAIL

GARDEN	WHEN TO VISIT	LOOK FOR

GARDENS TO VISIT

DATE VISITED	COMMENTS

GARDEN	WHEN TO VISIT	LOOK FOR

GARDENS TO VISIT

DATE VISITED	COMMENTS

NOTES

NOTES

NOTES

NOTES

NOTES

NOTES

NOTES

NOTES

NOTES

NOTES

NOTES